Now That You Are *His*

Dear Friend,

We rejoice with the commitment you have made to Jesus Christ. Please accept this book as our gift to you. May it encourage you to grow daily in your relationship with Jesus.

Pastor Zarlengo & the SGT Church Family
(631-265-2485)

"...be strong in the Lord and in the power of His might." Ephesians 6:10

Now That You Are His

First Steps in the Christian Walk

WITH COMPANION STUDY GUIDE

DAVID SHIBLEY

First printing: 1985
Eleventh printing: October 2011

New Leaf Press, P.O. Box 726, Green Forest, AR 72638
New Leaf Press is a division of the New Leaf Publishing Group, Inc.

ISBN: 978-0-89221-236-1
Library of Congress Catalog Number: 93-84142

Unless otherwise indicated, all Scripture quotations are taken from
the New King James Version, copyright © 1979, 1980, 1982 by
Thomas Nelson, Inc., Nashville, TN.

Cover design by Diana Bogardus

Please consider requesting that a copy of this volume be purchased
by your local library system.

Printed in the United States of America

Please visit our website for other great titles:
www.newleafpress.net

For information regarding author interviews, please contact the
publicity department at (870) 438-5288.

New Leaf Press
A Division of New Leaf Publishing Group

CONTENTS

Your Most Important Step

This book will help you take first steps in a life-long, growing relationship with Jesus Christ. If you have not met Jesus Christ in a commitment of your life and heart, now is the time to come to know Him. This step changes everything, for your life and for eternity.

The most important and most thrilling discovery in life is finding the way home to God. There are signposts that point us home to Him.

First, there is the signpost of *God's heart of love for you.* As the Creator of everything, God is perfect and holy. His heart of infinite love reaches out to embrace you. He desires to cleanse you of your sins. He longs to give you peace of mind and heart, purpose for living, and assurance of a home in heaven with Him.

The Bible says, "For God so loved the world that He gave His only begotten Son, that whoever believes in Him should not perish but have everlasting life" (John 3:16).

Jesus Christ offers you eternal life forever with Him in heaven. But He also offers you a full and abundant life right now. He said, "The thief [the devil] does not come except to steal, and to kill, and to destroy. I have come that they may have life, and that they may have it more abundantly" (John 10:10).

At this moment, God is reaching out in love to you. "In this is love, not that we loved God, but that He loved us and sent His Son to be the propitiation [sacrifice] for our sins" (1 John 4:10).

The second signpost is *your need for God.* The most desperate need of people everywhere is to be forgiven by God and restored to fellowship with Him. The mad pursuit after pleasure and possessions is often an unconscious search for God. Although we were created to enjoy His presence, humanity's rebellion against God's rule has cut our communion with Him. This rebellion is the root of all sin and has resulted in all the sadness in our world. All of our self-efforts to reach God have proved inadequate.

Our rebellion against God has separated us from Him. The Bible says, "Your iniquities have separated you from your God; and your sins have hidden His face from you" (Isaiah 59:2). This blight of sin has stretched over the entire human race. "All we like sheep have gone astray; we have turned, every one, to his own way; and the LORD has laid on Him the iniquity of us all" (Isaiah 53:6). "All have sinned and fall short of the glory of God" (Romans 3:23).

The payment for our sins is certain death and eternity without God. "The wages of sin is death, but the gift of God is eternal life in Christ Jesus our Lord" (Romans 6:23).

But the story doesn't end with your need.

Signpost number three is *God's provision for you — Jesus Christ.* While humanity raced madly toward judgment and doom, God intervened by sending Christ to pay for our sins.

Jesus Christ is God in human flesh. As the eternal Son of God, He lived a perfect, sinless life. His death is the sacrifice God accepts to pay for all your sins. Three days after His crucifixion He physically rose from the dead, forever triumphing over sin, death, and hell. As God's only provision for sin, He offers forgiveness and new life to you, right now. Jesus himself has said, "I am the way, the truth, and the life. No one comes to the Father except through Me" (John 14:6). Further, the Bible affirms that "there is one God and one Mediator between God and men, the Man Christ Jesus" (1 Timothy 2:5).

Eternal life is a free gift that God offers to you right now. This wonderful gift is provided, not because of what you have done, but because of what God has done for you. "For by grace you have been saved through faith, and that not of yourselves; it is the gift of God, not of works, lest anyone should boast" (Ephesians 2:8–9).

The proof of God's love for you is Christ's death for you on the cross. He died so you can experience the way home to God. "For Christ also suffered once for sins, the just for the unjust, that He might bring us to God " (1 Peter 3:18).

The fourth signpost is *your commitment to Christ.* What does it mean to commit yourself to Christ? First, it means repenting or turning away from your old way of living. In turning to Christ you must turn from all your sins and from all your efforts to save yourself. The Bible is clear that it is God who does the work in saving us. "Not by works of righteousness which we have done, but according to His mercy He saved us, through the washing of regeneration and renewing of the Holy Spirit" (Titus 3:5).

Also, this commitment means trusting fully in Jesus' death for you as the only payment ever needed for your sins. The Bible says, "As many as received Him, to them He gave the right to become children of God, to those who believe in His name" (John 1:12).

Since Christ has purchased you with His own blood, committing your life to Him also means transferring ownership of your life to Jesus Christ. Now there can be no other title for Him in your life than "Lord." Jesus Christ literally becomes your Master and you become His servant. When you come to Christ you take Him both as Savior and Lord. "If you confess with your mouth the Lord Jesus and believe in your heart that God has raised Him from the dead, you will be saved. For with the heart one believes unto righteousness, and with the mouth confession is made unto salvation. . . . For 'whoever calls on the name of the LORD shall be saved' " (Romans 10:9–13).

Now, what will you do with Jesus, this One who loved you enough to die in your place? You cannot be neutral about Him. He made it clear, "He who is not with Me is against Me, and he who does not gather with Me scatters abroad" (Matthew 12:30).

Now is the time for you to repent of your sins and commit your life to Jesus Christ. To repent means to turn away completely from all our sins and all attempts to save ourselves. "Behold, now is the accepted time; behold, now is the day of salvation" (2 Corinthians 6:2).

You can come to Christ wherever you are, right now. As you receive Him, He will receive you. You will finally and eternally be "home," at peace with God. The past will be forgotten. Your sins will be forgiven. A new life will begin for you right now. "Therefore, if anyone is in Christ, he is a new creation; old things have passed away; behold, all things have become new" (2 Corinthians 5:17).

Make this the prayer of your heart to God right now: *"Lord Jesus, thank You for dying on the cross for me. Right now I repent of my sins and trust Your shed blood as the full payment for all my sins. I believe You are the Son of God and that God has raised You from the dead. I now receive You as my personal Savior. I commit my life completely to You as my Lord. Thank You for hearing my prayer, forgiving my sins, and coming into my life as You promised. Amen."*

If you prayed this prayer in sincerity and faith, welcome to the family of God! Jesus Christ has promised to come into your life when, in repentance and faith, you invite Him to be your Lord. The Bible says, "And this is the testimony: that God has given us eternal life, and this life is in His Son. He who has the Son has life; he who does not have the Son of God does not have life" (1 John 5:11–12). The Son of God now lives in you. You now have eternal life.

This book is dedicated to helping you grow as a follower of Jesus. Now that you are His, I encourage you to take these important first steps that will help lead you to a life of fruitfulness and fulfillment in your walk with the Lord.

STEP ONE

Publicly Confess
Your Faith in Christ

Congratulations! You have made the most important and most thrilling discovery in life. Nothing is more wonderful than establishing a personal relationship with God. This relationship began the moment you put your faith in Jesus Christ. By turning from your sins and committing your life to Jesus Christ as your Savior and Lord, you have begun an entirely new life.

You are proof positive that the age of miracles has not passed because a miracle — the miracle of a new birth — has happened to you. This transfer of ownership is so life-transforming that Jesus referred to it as being *born again*. This is one of several terms the Bible uses in reference to your experience of coming to know Jesus Christ in a personal way. Your first birth was a physical birth. But now you also have experienced a spiritual birth. Jesus said, "That which is born of the flesh is flesh, and that which is born of the Spirit is spirit. Do not marvel that I said to you, 'You must be born again' " (John 3:6–7). Now, not only is your body alive, but your spirit — the inner person — is alive, as well. You have been made "alive to God in Christ Jesus our Lord" (Romans 6:11).

The Bible also refers to your new condition of being in Christ as being *saved*. You have been saved from the penalty of your sins, which would have been eternity without God and without hope. Those without Christ already live under condemnation for their sins. Jesus, referring to himself, said, "He who believes in Him is not condemned; but he who does not believe is condemned already, because he has not believed in the name of the only begotten Son of God" (John 3:18).

Most people would agree that every person has committed some wrong. The Bible clearly says, "All have sinned and fall short of the glory of God" (Romans 3:23). Sin must be paid for. The punishment for sin is death and separation from God. Either you must pay for your sins yourself or trust the payment that was made in your behalf when Jesus shed His blood for you. The Bible says, "The wages [payment] of sin is death, but the gift of God is eternal life in Christ Jesus our Lord" (Romans 6:23).

Because you have put your faith and confidence in what Christ has done for you, you will be saved from that coming day when God judges unbelievers for their sin and unbelief. This is the awesome day when Jesus will return "in flaming fire taking vengeance on those who do not know God, and on those who do not obey the gospel of our Lord Jesus Christ. These shall be punished with everlasting destruction from the presence of the Lord and from the glory of His power, when He comes, in that Day, to be glorified in His saints and to be admired among all those who believe" (2 Thessalonians 1:8–10).

But the Bible assures you, "If you confess with your mouth the Lord Jesus and believe in your heart that God has raised Him from the dead, you will be saved" (Romans 10:9). Have you done that? Have you confessed the living Christ as your Savior? Then the Bible says salvation is yours!

Remember, it is God who does the saving. We are the grateful recipients of the work He has done. "Not by works of righteousness which we have done, but according to His mercy He saved us, through the washing of regeneration and renewing of the Holy Spirit" (Titus 3:5).

The Bible also declares that you have been *redeemed* — purchased from the control of Satan and sin. Jesus Christ has literally paid for you you with His blood. "Knowing that you were not redeemed with corruptible things, like silver or gold, from your aimless conduct received by tradition from your fathers, but with the precious blood of Christ, as of a lamb without blemish and without spot" (1 Peter 1:18–19).

Because Christ has purchased you, He is your rightful owner. As your owner, He should be free to control every area of your life. Suppose you were to go to a car dealer and pay cash for a new car. The dealer receives your money, promising to give you the car in return. But when he comes back, he only gives you the steering wheel, a couple of tires, and the brakes. What would you say? You would probably tell him, "Look, I paid the full price for this car. I have the right to demand the full product!" So it is with Christ. He paid the full price for you. He has the right to demand the full product of your life. Nothing is to be kept back from His control. Since He created you, He knows best how you should live. "For you were bought at a price; therefore glorify God in your body and in your spirit, which are God's" (1 Corinthians 6:20).

The Bible also teaches that you have been *converted.* To be converted means to be changed. You, my friend, have been changed. Once you were lost, now you are saved. Once you were alienated from God, now you are His child. Once you were on the road to judgment and hell, now you are going to heaven. Once you thought you could make it on your own, now you know you need Jesus. That is why Jesus said, "Unless you are converted and become as little children, you will by no means enter the kingdom of heaven" (Matthew 18:3).

You Can Be Sure

One of the cruelest attacks the devil hurls at new believers is his attempt to make them doubt their salvation. "Maybe I didn't say the right words." "What if I wasn't sincere enough?" "Can I really live the Christian life?" "What if I sin?" Satan tries to haunt people with these and a thousand other little barbs of doubt.

But, thank God, there is a way to full assurance. You need never doubt your salvation. You don't have to give in to fear or doubt.

Remember this: *The ultimate assurance of your salvation is that Jesus Christ lives inside of you.* Since you have made this commitment of your life to Christ, the Bible says that Christ now lives in you. Jesus has made a wonderful promise to all who receive Him. He promised, "Behold, I stand at the door [of your life] and knock. If anyone hears My voice and opens the door, I will come in to him" (Revelation 3:20).

Have you done that? Have you opened the door of your life to Jesus? Then where is Jesus? He has come to live inside of you! That's His promise to you. Think of it! Jesus Christ actually lives inside of you by His Spirit. His life inside of you is your guarantee of salvation and eternal life. The Bible says, "And this is the testimony: that God has given us eternal life, and this life is in His Son. He who has the Son has life; he who does not have the Son of God does not have life" (1 John 5:11–12).

"But," you may be saying, "you don't know some of the terrible things I've done. How can God accept me after what I've done?" Remember, God doesn't accept you on the basis of what you have or have not done. He accepts you on the basis of what *He* has done for you on the cross. He accepts you because Christ, the holy One, lives in you. Christ is in you and you are in Christ. When you receive Christ as your Lord and Savior, you are put in the secure place of being "in Christ." God accepts you because Christ is in you and you are in Him. The Bible says that "He has made us accepted in the Beloved [Jesus Christ]" (Ephesians 1:6).

The devil knows you will never grow much in your relationship with Christ if you fear that your salvation is in jeopardy. But don't let him defeat you with doubts. You are not on probation with God. He has not only given you life, but He has also given you *eternal* life. You have been born into His family and you cannot be "un-birthed." You have been "born again, not of corruptible seed but incorruptible, through the word of God which lives and abides forever" (1 Peter 1:23).

The Bible is clear that you are saved by the grace of God. This means that God, because of His infinite love, saves us when we put our trust in Christ, even though we do not merit or deserve His favor. "For by grace you have been saved through faith, and that not of yourselves; it is the gift of God, not of works, lest anyone should boast" (Ephesians 2:8–9).

When you get to heaven, you will not see anyone boasting about how he deserves to be there because of his good life. No, everyone in heaven will know they are there only because of God's amazing grace. In gratitude to God for His wonderful salvation, you will want to live a life that is pleasing to Him. "For the grace of God that brings salvation has appeared to all men, teaching us that, denying ungodliness and worldly lusts, we should live soberly, righteously, and godly in the present age" (Titus 2:11–12).

As a young child in Vacation Bible School, I trusted Christ as my Savior. Since that day, I have never seriously doubted my relationship with Him. I believe the reason is that from those early days my parents and teachers helped me see that my security rested, not in my attempts to hold onto Jesus, but in the settled fact that He is holding onto me.

Perhaps you have been plagued with doubt from time to time. Let me give you three simple steps to bring you a confident assurance of your salvation.

First, realize that *salvation is not your accomplishment but His accomplishment.* As the old hymn says, "Jesus paid it all. All to Him I owe." What more could be added to the blood that Jesus has spilt for you? You must be persuaded, as Paul was, that Jesus is perfectly capable of protecting and keeping what He has purchased. "For I know whom I have believed and am persuaded that He is able to keep what I have committed to Him until that Day" (2 Timothy 1:12).

It is God who does the saving. Therefore, your salvation does not depend upon your strength but upon His strength. Salvation is not something you do, it is something God has done for you. All the religions of the world begin with do's and don'ts. But biblical Christianity begins with *done!* On the cross Jesus cried, "It is finished!" (John 19:30). The price for your salvation has been paid in full. Now you can know you are saved, not only because you have given your life to Jesus, but because Jesus has given His life for you.

Second, *trust God's promises to you.* God is perfect in all His ways. God not only will not lie to you, but the Bible also says He cannot lie. Because of your faith in Christ, you now have "eternal life which God, who cannot lie, promised before time began" (Titus 1:2).

No person has ever been as trustworthy as Jesus Christ. And it is Jesus himself who has promised, "Most assuredly, I say to you, he who hears My word and believes in Him who sent Me has everlasting life, and shall not come into judgment, but has passed from death into life" (John 5:24).

Again, He has promised, "I am the door. If anyone enters by Me, he will be saved, and will go in and out and find pasture" (John 10:9).

Still again He has assured you, "And I give them eternal life, and they shall never perish; neither shall anyone snatch them out of My hand. My Father, who has given them to Me, is greater than all; and no one is able to snatch them out of My Father's hand" (John 10:28–29). And still another time He promises, "I will never leave you nor forsake you" (Hebrews 13:5).

So put your confidence in God, who cannot lie, and in His word which endures forever.

Third, *don't trust your feelings.* Perhaps the two most change-able things in life are the weather and human emotions. One minute you can be on the mountaintop of exhilaration and the next minute in the valley of despair. Many times our emotions are subject to the circumstances surrounding us. How tragic, then, if your faith rests in how you feel at any particular moment rather than in God. Your hope of salvation simply cannot rest on how you feel at any given moment. Rather, your hope of eternal life must be squarely planted in this settled fact of history — Jesus Christ died for you and rose again.

Of course, there will be times when your heart thrills at the presence of Jesus. This is a good thing. I'm not saying that your faith should be void of emotion. On the contrary, any healthy relationship includes our emotions and you have entered into a relationship with Jesus. I'm simply saying that you cannot depend on your feelings for the assurance of salvation. So when in doubt, doubt your doubts and trust the promises of God.

You Are a New Person

The rate of growth for every Christian is different. Some new believers seem to grow rapidly while others seem to grow slowly but surely. But you can be certain of this: You *will* grow. Every created thing, both in the plant and in the animal kingdoms, grows if it is alive. So it is with you. You have been made alive in Jesus Christ. And because there is new life in you, you will grow.

You may already be discovering something fascinating and exciting happening to you. You are beginning to think differently. You are beginning to act differently. Things you once hated you now love. Things you once loved you now despise. Whereas once you were tolerant and accepting of sin, now you reject it. Whereas once you were indifferent or even hostile to spiritual things, now you "hunger and thirst for righteousness" (Matthew 5:6). Indeed, you are a new person. "Therefore, if anyone is in Christ, he is a new creation; old things have passed away; behold, all things have become new" (2 Corinthians 5:17).

Not only have you changed, but you are also continuing to change. God will continue His work in your life. His ultimate purpose in bringing you into His family is to make you Christ-like.

Now you can rejoice that every circumstance of life will be used by God to bring about this transformation of your life into the image of Christ. No matter what happens to you, you can know that God's purpose behind it is to make you more like Jesus. "And we know that all things work together for good to those who love God, to those who are the called according to His purpose. For whom He foreknew, He also predestined to be conformed to the image of His Son, that He might be the firstborn among many brethren" (Romans 8:28–29).

The moment you come to Christ a wonderful transaction takes place. God forgives your sin. "And you, being dead in your trespasses and the uncircumcision of your flesh [the old way of living], He has made alive together with Him, having forgiven you all trespasses" (Colossians 2:13). God puts His righteousness in you, "even the righteousness of God, through faith in Jesus Christ, to all and on all who believe" (Romans 3:22). God makes you forever His child. "But as many as received Him, to them He gave the right to become children of God, even to those who believe in His name" (John 1:12).

You Have a New Destiny

God has taken you on as a lifetime project. From now on you will be aware of His presence in your life, ever seeking to bless you, strengthen you, and conform you into the very image of Christ. Although life will continue to have its problems, you have met the Problem-solver.

Some people seem to have the idea that if a person becomes a Christian all the joy and excitement will be stripped out of life. This is one of the devil's most ridiculous lies. Nothing could be further from the truth. When a person comes to Christ, that's when the excitement really begins. Those who have no relationship with God seek joy and, at best, only find surface happiness. But a Christian in fellowship with his Lord has the deep-seated joy of knowing that he has found meaning for his life. He has the anchored peace of knowing his sins are forgiven and covered by the blood of Christ. He has the profound thrill of participating in God's lofty purposes in the earth.

Because Christ is in you, you have the promise of abundant life now and eternal life with Him in heaven. Jesus said, "The thief [the devil] does not come except to steal, and to kill, and to destroy. I have come that they may have life, and that they may have it more abundantly" (John 10:10). As you live in fellowship with Christ, your life will be full, meaningful, and abundant.

In Christ, you have both abundant life and eternal life. Yes, eternal life means that you will live forever with the Lord in heaven. But to have eternal life also means that you have the very life of God living in you right now. The life of God, the uncreated One without beginning and without end, is now in you. Just imagine! Because you belong to Christ, God's life is now coursing through you.

So welcome to the adventure! The God of the universe has staked His claim on you. And He will continue His loving, transforming work in you until all of His designs for you and through you are completed. You can be sure of it. "Being confident of this very thing, that He who has begun a good work in you will complete it until the day of Jesus Christ" (Philippians 1:6).

The Importance of a Public Confession

Have you noticed that important transitions and transactions in life are almost always made publicly? Graduation is a transition that is declared publicly. Marriage is a transition that is declared publicly. Even the mergers of companies are publicly announced. Yet, as important as these events are, they are not as important for this life or the life to come as the transition out of death into life that occurs when you receive Christ as your Lord and Savior. This most important of all of life's decisions should certainly be declared publicly.

Whenever Jesus challenged someone to follow Him, He always called that person publicly. In this way, Jesus stressed the importance of a clear-cut commitment to Him. By publicly declaring your faith in Christ, you announce to the world that you are not ashamed to claim Jesus Christ as your Lord. Also, this public confession of faith helps seal your decision for Christ in your own heart and mind.

You should confess Christ publicly for a number of reasons. First, your public declaration of loyalty to Christ puts your faith on the line. By making a public confession of your faith in Jesus Christ you pass a "point of no return." You are proclaiming to a watching world that you are devoted, now and forever, to Jesus Christ.

Second, this public confession of faith helps to seal your decision for Christ in your own heart and mind. Jesus said, "Out of the abundance of the heart the mouth speaks" (Matthew 12:34). As a natural response, you will express outwardly what God has done inwardly.

Third, your acknowledgment of Jesus publicly encourages you that He will one day publicly acknowledge you. Jesus promised, "Whoever confesses Me before men, him I will confess before My Father who is in heaven. But whoever denies Me before men, him I will also deny before My Father who is in heaven" (Matthew 10:32–33).

If you have not already done so, take this first step of obedience and publicly declare your faith in Christ. Attend a church this week where an opportunity will be given for you to make a public confession of your faith in Jesus Christ as your Savior and Lord.

To help mark your progress in taking these steps, put a check (x) in the boxes when you have taken each step of growth.

TAKE A STEP OF ACTION!

❏ I have publicly stated that I am trusting Jesus Christ as my Savior and I am following Him as my Lord.

❏ Remember: "If you confess with your mouth the Lord Jesus and believe in your heart that God has raised Him from the dead, you will be saved. For with the heart one believes unto righteousness, and with the mouth confession is made unto salvation" (Romans 10:9–10).

STEP TWO

Follow Christ in Water Baptism

When Jesus commissioned His followers to make the nations His disciples, He told them to baptize in water all who would follow Him. He commanded them, "All authority has been given to Me in heaven and on earth. Go therefore and make disciples of all the nations, baptizing them in the name of the Father and of the Son and of the Holy Spirit" (Matthew 28:18–19). Through the centuries, water baptism has been one of the clearest declarations a believer can make of his allegiance to Jesus Christ.

Now that you are His, you will want to obey this clear command of the Lord. Jesus said, "If you love Me, keep My commandments" (John 14:15). Obedience to Christ not only proves your sincerity, but it is also one of the secrets of experiencing continual joy in the Lord. In reference to obeying His teachings, Jesus said, "If you know these things, blessed are you if you do them" (John 13:17).

Water baptism is called an "ordinance" of the church because it is something Jesus ordained for those who follow Him. In fact, baptism was the normal way in which new believers gave public confession of their faith in Christ in Bible times. No Christian in those days would have even considered omitting this step of obedience. "And he commanded them to be baptized in the name of the Lord" (Acts 10:48).

Since Jesus himself was baptized in water, we as His followers should gladly follow our Lord's example. Also, throughout the New Testament the Apostles instructed new believers to be baptized in water.

Crucified with Christ

The good news of the gospel is that Christ has been crucified for you. But that's only part of the wonderful story. Not only has Christ been crucified for you, but the Bible also teaches that you have been crucified with Christ. All of your old thought patterns, unclean desires, and sinful actions were put to death on the cross of Christ. Now you are to "reckon yourselves to be dead indeed to sin, but alive to God in Christ Jesus our Lord" (Romans 6:11).

This is a great truth that every Christian should grasp. Your old life has been put to death! Now you are living a new life — the very life of Christ in and through you. Now that you are His, you can affirm, "I have been crucified with Christ; it is no longer I who live, but Christ lives in me; and the life which I now live in the flesh I live by faith in the Son of God, who loved me and gave Himself for me" (Galatians 2:20).

Before you came to Christ, the Bible describes your condition as "dead in trespasses." When you repented of your sins and received Jesus Christ as your Savior and Lord, you were made alive in Christ.

> And you He made alive, who were dead in trespasses and sins, in which you once walked according to the course of this world, according to the prince of the power of the air, the spirit who now works in the sons of disobedience, among whom also we all once conducted ourselves in the lusts of our flesh, fulfilling the desires of the flesh and of the mind, and were by nature children of wrath, just as the others. But God, who is rich in mercy, because of His great love with which He loved us, even when we were dead in trespasses, made us alive together with Christ (by grace you have been saved) (Ephesians 2:1–5).

You have been crucified with Christ and raised to new life in Him. Your baptism in water becomes an affirmation and reference point of this wonderful reality. Since water baptism nearly always took place almost immediately after a person was saved, the Bible speaks of this experience as one continuum. "Therefore we were buried with Him through baptism into death, that just as Christ was raised from the dead by the glory of the Father, even so we also should walk in newness of life" (Romans 6:4).

The Significance of Baptism

Throughout the New Testament it is striking that water baptism was only administered to those who had voluntarily put their faith in Christ for salvation. Therefore, water baptism is for Christian believers only. The word "to baptize" in the original language of the New Testament carries the idea of being placed completely under the water. The mode of baptism should not be a point of contention among Christians. However, we believe that in keeping with the symbolic beauty of the burial of the old way of life, baptism should be by immersion.

Your baptism is very significant as a statement of faith. First, by baptism you are stating your faith that you have died to the old life and have been made a new person in Christ. By going down under the water and coming out again, you are giving a vivid visual aid to those watching. It helps them understand the good news that you have been made alive and new in Jesus Christ.

Second, your baptism is a statement of your faith in the burial and resurrection of Jesus Christ. Again, the picture of immersion helps us to understand the basic truth of the Gospel that "Christ died for our sins according to the Scriptures, and that He was buried, and that He rose again the third day according to the Scriptures" (1 Corinthians 15:3-4).

Also, your baptism testifies to your faith in your personal future resurrection. By baptism you are saying that, should you die before Jesus returns to earth, you know He will raise your body to live with Him forever when He comes again.

A Sign to the World

The Bible says that there are three witnesses on earth to your salvation. "And there are three that bear witness on earth: the Spirit, the water, and the blood; and these three agree as one" (1 John 5:8). The Holy Spirit bears witness to your own heart that you are God's child. The blood of Christ, applied to you by faith when you came to Christ, bears witness to God that you belong to Him. And the water — the waters of baptism — bears witness to the world that you are God's child.

In many cultures around the world, a Christian's baptism is seen by non-believers as even more significant than the Christian's initial confession of faith. Many times non-Christians think that a new convert can be persuaded to return to his old life before his baptism. But in many parts of the world, if a new believer is baptized in water, this signals his official break with the old life and his public declaration of himself as a true follower of Jesus. Upon baptism, attempts to persuade the new Christian to return to the old life are often terminated and sometimes even a funeral for the new Christian is given. This shows how seriously the event of water baptism is viewed by the unbelieving world.

Since this is so, your baptism is a great opportunity to share your faith in Christ with your family and friends. Invite them to witness your baptism. Then, perhaps you could invite them over for dinner or refreshments to share your joy. This is one of the finest testimonies you can give to loved ones you want to see converted to Christ.

As you anticipate your own baptism, prepare yourself for a very meaningful step in your Christian walk. Many times special gifts and blessings from the Holy Spirit accompany water baptism. So come expecting God's Spirit to minister powerfully to you through your baptism.

TAKE A STEP OF ACTION!

❐ I have been baptized in water as a testimony to the world of my union with Christ.

❐ Remember: "Therefore we were buried with Him through baptism into death, that just as Christ was raised from the dead by the glory of the Father, even so we also should walk in newness of life" (Romans 6:4).

STEP THREE

Allow the Holy Spirit to Fill and Control You

Aperson can breathe without air as easily as a Christian can live without the Holy Spirit." These forceful words by 19th-century evangelist D.L. Moody clearly remind us of our need of the presence and power of the Holy Spirit.

The Holy Spirit is God actively involved in our world today. Jesus referred to the Holy Spirit as the "Comforter" He would send to help and encourage us. When you received Christ as your Lord and Savior, the Holy Spirit came to reside in you. It is the Holy Spirit who gives us power to live a life that pleases God.

The Ministry of the Holy Spirit

The central work of the Holy Spirit is to point people to Jesus Christ. Before you came to Christ, the Holy Spirit was actively drawing you to Him. Now that you are His, the Holy Spirit continues to work — now from the inside — to keep you centered on the Lord Jesus. It is the Holy Spirit who convicts the non-Christian of his need of Christ. Concerning this work of the Spirit, Jesus said, "And when He has come, He will convict the world of sin, and of righteousness, and of judgment" (John 16:8).

It is the Holy Spirit who guides believers into an ever-deepening relationship with the Lord. Jesus said, "When He, the Spirit of truth, has come, He will guide you into all truth; for He will not speak on His own authority, but whatever He hears He will speak; and He will tell you things to come. He will glorify Me, for He will take of what is Mine and declare it to you" (John 16:13–14).

It is the Holy Spirit who produces the very character of Jesus in and through you. "But the fruit of the Spirit is love, joy, peace, long-suffering, kindness, goodness, faithfulness, gentleness, self control. Against such there is no law" (Galatians 5:22–23).

There are two ways to attempt to live the Christian life. One is to try by your own strength to live for Jesus. The other is to allow the Holy Spirit to live the life of Jesus through you! If you "try" in your own ability to produce this fruit of Jesus' character, you will only become frustrated. But if you allow the Holy Spirit to produce His fruit in you, then you will enter into a joyful walk of trusting and yielding to the control of God's life-giving Spirit.

Not only does the Holy Spirit produce the fruit of Jesus in us, but He also gifts Christians with special enablements. These gifts of the Spirit are listed in three passages in the Bible. Ephesians 4 speaks of specially gifted people whom Jesus has given to the church by His Spirit: apostles, prophets, evangelists, pastors, and teachers. Romans 12 chronicles the spiritual gifts of prophecy, faith, the ministry of helps, teaching, exhortation, giving, and mercy. In 1 Corinthians 12 there is a list of the spiritual gifts of the word of wisdom, the word of knowledge, faith, healing, miracles, prophecy, discerning of spirits, tongues, and interpretation of tongues.

These gifts are given to Christians today to strengthen the Church and provide supernatural power to build up believers and reach the entire world with the good news of Jesus Christ.

Your Key to Power

Just before He ascended into heaven, Jesus encouraged His followers, "But you shall receive power when the Holy Spirit has come upon you; and you shall be witnesses to Me in Jerusalem, and in all Judea and Samaria, and to the end of the earth" (Acts 1:8). Soon after this commission the disciples came together to pray and wait for the promised Holy Spirit and His power. Then it happened: "When the Day of Pentecost had fully come, they were all with one accord in one place. And suddenly there came a sound from heaven, as of a rushing mighty wind, and it filled the whole house where they were sitting. Then there appeared to them divided tongues, as of fire, and one sat upon each of them. And they were all filled with the Holy Spirit and began to speak with other tongues, as the Spirit gave them utterance" (Acts 2:1–4).

As a result of being filled with the Holy Spirit, they reached the entire known world with the gospel of Christ and began the mightiest movement in human history — the church of the Lord Jesus Christ.

This same power is available to you today. It is God's desire for you to be a joyful, bold witness for Jesus Christ. He has provided the Holy Spirit to empower your life and witness.

Be Filled with the Spirit

There is no way to live an abundant Christian life apart from being controlled by the Holy Spirit. The Bible says, "And do not be drunk with wine, in which is dissipation; but be filled with the Spirit, speaking to one another in psalms and hymns and spiritual songs, singing and making melody in your heart to the Lord, giving thanks always for all things to God the Father in the name of our Lord Jesus Christ, submitting to one another in the fear of God" (Ephesians 5:18–21).

To be filled with the Spirit is to allow Him to control you, giving you supernatural power for witness and ministry. In Ephesians 5, this experience is described as being filled with the Spirit. It is also referred to in the Bible as being "baptized" in the Holy Spirit. This carries the idea of being completely immersed in the life of the Spirit. Referring to their coming experience on the Day of Pentecost, Jesus told those early believers, "John truly baptized with water, but you shall be baptized with the Holy Spirit not many days from now" (Acts 1:5).

Have you been filled with the Holy Spirit? Can you look back on a time when you allowed the Holy Spirit to control your life with no reservations? Are you allowing God's Spirit supreme control in your life today? If not, you can experience the fullness of the Spirit right now. It is God's desire to fill your life with His presence and power — beginning now!

Martin Luther said, "It is not so important how the Holy Spirit comes to us. What is important is how we come to the Holy Spirit." As you anticipate this wonderful experience, first, prepare your heart by desiring the Holy Spirit to fill you. Jesus promised, "Blessed are those who hunger and thirst for righteousness, for they shall be filled" (Matthew 5:6).

Second, turn from every sin in your life. Renounce all evil attitudes and practices and come before the Lord, trusting His blood to cleanse you from every sin. The Holy Spirit only fills clean, empty vessels.

Now, in renewed consecration of your life to the Lord, give control of every area of your life to the Lord Jesus. Then invite the Holy Spirit to take control. Simply ask the Holy Spirit to fill you. Jesus promised, "If you then, being evil, know how to give good gifts to your children, how much more will your heavenly Father give the Holy Spirit to those who ask Him!" (Luke 11:13).

You will begin to sense a wonderful joy welling up within you, deep in your spirit. Give vent to that by opening your mouth in praise to God. Allow the rivers of living water to sweep over you as you praise the Lord. Jesus said, "'He who believes in Me, as the Scripture has said, out of his heart will flow rivers of living water.' But this He spoke concerning the Spirit, whom those believing in Him would receive" (John 7:38–39).

In several of the instances recorded in the Book of Acts, the Scriptures say when they were filled or baptized in the Holy Spirit, they spoke in tongues. As your praises well up within you to God, you can allow this God-given language of prayer and praise to be expressed as you open your mouth in praise to God.

Now, wherever you are, allow the Holy Spirit to fill and control you. Then remember, to be filled with the Spirit is not simply an experience. It is a way of life — an abundant life under the Spirit's gracious control.

TAKE A STEP OF ACTION!

❏ I have asked the Holy Spirit to fill and control me. By faith, I now receive His fullness.

❏ Remember: "And do not be drunk with wine, in which is dissipation; but be filled with the Spirit" (Ephesians 5:18).

STEP FOUR

Turn from Every Known Sin

S in cuts fellowship with God. Nothing could be more serious for the Christian than attempting to live outside of His
fellowship and presence. Further, sin cuts the joy out of life. The
devil attempts to steal everything precious in life from us. He
does this by trying to draw us into sin. Jesus said, "The thief [the
devil] does not come except to steal, and to kill, and to destroy.
I have come that they may have life, and that they may have it
more abundantly" (John 10:10).

The apostle James wrote, "Let no one say when he is tempted,
'I am tempted by God'; for God cannot be tempted by evil, nor
does He Himself tempt anyone. But each one is tempted when
he is drawn away by his own desires and enticed. Then, when
desire has conceived, it gives birth to sin; and sin, when it is full-
grown, brings forth death" (James 1:13–15).

Temptation is a fact of life. But you no longer have to give way to temptation. It is possible to live a life of victory over sin. The victory comes by understanding your union with Jesus Christ.

Your New Nature

Now that you are His, you have a new nature, the very nature of Christ. Although the tug to sin will continue, sin no longer has any dominion over you. The old nature of sin was crucified with Christ. This became real in your personal life when you were born again.

The driving force of sin, your old nature, was dealt a death blow at Calvary. Now we no longer serve sin; we serve Jesus Christ. We are no longer the slaves either of sin or of dead religion (what the Bible calls "the law"). "For when we were in the flesh, the sinful passions which were aroused by the law were at work in our members to bear fruit to death. But now we have been delivered from the law, having died to what we were held by, so that we should serve in the newness of the Spirit and not in the oldness of the letter" (Romans 7:5–6).

When we received Christ as our Lord and Savior, He literally took up residence in us by His Spirit. That is why this new nature is referred to as "the Spirit" — the new nature within us that desires to please God. In fact, it is the very nature of Jesus Christ. Therefore, it is no longer a question of my straining and trying to please God. Rather, it is a question of whether or not I will release the Christ-life, the life of the Spirit, in me.

Chapters 6 through 8 of Romans frame the classic passage dealing with this battle of the Spirit versus the flesh. After encouraging believers to understand their union with Jesus Christ, Paul reminds us that a holy life cannot be achieved simply by trying to obey God's law, as holy as that law is. A holy life is only possible by walking in the Spirit.

"For what the law could not do in that it was weak through the flesh, God did by sending His own Son in the likeness of sinful flesh, on account of sin: He condemned sin in the flesh, that the righteous requirement of the law might be fulfilled in us who do not walk according to the flesh but according to the Spirit. For those who live according to the flesh set their minds on the things of the flesh, but those who live according to the Spirit, the things of the Spirit. For to be carnally minded is death, but to be spiritually minded is life and peace" (Romans 8:3–6).

Now we are truly free. We are free — not to do wrong, but to do right! We are now liberated from the power of sin to live lives pleasing to God.

As we feed the new nature by prayer, the Word, fellowship with other believers, and witness by our words and actions, this new life of the Spirit grows strong and prevails. So there is a simple remedy for victory over temptation: "Walk in the Spirit, and you shall not fulfill the lust of the flesh" (Galatians 5:16).

Relationship and Fellowship

Nothing could be more wonderful than to have this secure, loving relationship with your Heavenly Father. As it is in a human relationship between a father and child, so your *relationship* with your Heavenly Father is secure, but your *fellowship* with Him can be broken by sin.

I deeply desire for my two sons to grow up into strong, well-adjusted adults. I know then that it is vital for me to continually assure them of my love for them. I must remind them that my love for them is unconditional; that it cannot be diminished by their actions, either good or bad. I must tell them that, whether they humiliate me or make me proud of them, their name will always be "Shibley." They are mine. Nothing can change that. Nor would I want it changed because I love them. I will own them as my sons, no matter what happens.

Of course, this does not mean that they can have the same level of intimacy and fellowship with me, whether or not they obey me. When they obey me , we live in harmony and fellowship. When they disobey me, although my love for them remains the same, our fellowship and intimacy are broken. Our fellowship can only be restored as they ask my forgiveness for their disobedience and determine to walk in obedience to me in the future. I may decide to discipline them for their rebellion but even this demonstrates my love for them.

After all, if the boy down the street does something wrong, it is very unlikely that I will discipline him. You see, he isn't my child. But if my sons disobey, that's a different matter. I have a vested interest in how my children turn out. And so it is with your Heavenly Father. He loves you with an everlasting love. You are His child. He is your Father. Your relationship is secure. But your fellowship with your Father will be determined by whether or not you obey Him.

As with the relationship of any good father with his children, we sometimes need correction. But even His correction is an indication of His love for us. "My son, do not despise the chastening of the LORD, nor be discouraged when you are rebuked by Him; for whom the LORD loves He chastens, and scourges every son whom He receives" (Hebrews 12:5–6).

Spiritual Breathing

When you disobey the will of your Father in heaven, there is a way to be immediately and fully restored to fellowship with

Him. Because He loves you, He wants to have fellowship with you. It is sin that cuts fellowship with God. It is repentance, or turning from sin, that restores fellowship with God.

This is what the Bible means when it speaks of confessing our sins. To confess means to agree with God concerning your sin; to agree with Him that sin is to have no place in your life as a Christian who loves the Lord. When you turn from your sins to God, He readily forgives you and restores your fellowship with Him. "If we confess our sins, He is faithful and just to forgive us our sins and to cleanse us from all unrighteousness" (1 John 1:9).

Dr. Bill Bright, founder of Campus Crusade for Christ, referred to this as "spiritual breathing" — breathing out the bad by confessing our sins to God, then breathing in His forgiveness and restoration. In this way you can keep short accounts with God, consistently walking in His forgiveness and power.

When You Are Tempted

Temptation is not sin. Yielding to the temptation is. Remember, sin is an attitude of rebellion against God. Sin begins in the mind and it is defeated in the mind, as well.

Paul gave the formula for victory over temptation in Romans 6. The first step is to *know* that your old nature has been crucified with Christ. "Knowing this, that our old man was crucified with Him, that the body of sin might be done away with, that we should no longer be slaves of sin" (Romans 6:6).

The second step is to *reckon*, or count on the fact that because your old nature is dead and buried, it will never rule over you again. "Likewise you also, reckon yourselves to be dead indeed to sin, but alive to God in Christ Jesus our Lord" (Romans 6:11).

Then *yield* your entire person — body, soul, and spirit — to God. "Therefore do not let sin reign in your mortal body, that you should obey it in its lusts. And do not present your members as instruments of unrighteousness to sin, but present yourselves to God as being alive from the dead, and your members as instruments of righteousness to God" (Romans 6:12–13).

As you understand and live out these truths you too will be able to say, "I have been crucified with Christ; it is no longer I who live, but Christ lives in me; and the life which I now live in the flesh I live by faith in the Son of God, who loved me and gave Himself for me" (Galatians 2:20).

TAKE A STEP OF ACTION!

❐ I have turned away from all known sin and, by faith, I now receive God's cleansing and forgiveness.

❐ Remember: "If we confess our sins, He is faithful and just to forgive us our sins and to cleanse us from all unrighteousness" (1 John 1:9).

STEP FIVE

Unite with a Strong Local Church

Some time ago a friend was telling me of his disappointment with the churches he had visited. "I'm looking for the perfect church," he said.

"If you find it," I joked, "please don't join it. You'd ruin it!"

You see, as long as we imperfect humans make up churches, churches will be less than perfect. However, this is no reason to dismiss the Church. The Church is ordained and instituted by God himself. The true Church is comprised of all those who have repented of their sins and committed their lives to Jesus Christ. But this global Church expresses itself in local, visible groups of believers.

The apostle Paul urged the leaders of the church at Ephesus, "Take heed to yourselves and to all the flock, among which the Holy Spirit has made you overseers, to shepherd the church of

God which He purchased with His own blood" (Acts 20:28). Because of the invaluable price that was paid for the Church's redemption, the Church is of utmost value to God. It should be to you as well.

The Need for Fellowship

The need for a strong local church in your life cannot be over-emphasized. The day of the "Lone Ranger Christian" who tries to live the Christian life in a vacuum is over. I was in college when the Jesus Movement of the late sixties and early seventies was in full swing. Time and again I heard expressions like, "Jesus, yes! Church, no!" Many were quick to point out the imperfections of the Church.

Yet where are the "Jesus people" today? No one doubts that most of the Jesus people had a deep love for Christ. But because so many of them failed to appreciate Christ's body, the Church, they have been strewn along the roadsides of life, no longer fruitful for Jesus Christ.

It would be impossible for you to call yourself my friend and not also highly esteem my wife. In the same way, it is impossible to feign allegiance to Jesus and disregard His bride. In the great passage on Christian marriage in Ephesians 5, Paul says, "For we are members of His body, of His flesh and of His bones. 'For this reason a man shall leave his father and mother and be joined to his wife, and the two shall become one flesh.' This is a great mystery, but I speak concerning Christ and the church" (Ephesians 5:30–32). Christ's love of the Church is likened to the sacrificial love of a husband for his bride.

When you think of "the Church," you should not think of a building of bricks and mortar. Under the new covenant, because of the blood of Jesus, redeemed people are the Church, not the buildings where they meet. Actually, Christians do not build sanctuaries, we *are* sanctuaries. God dwells in us by His Spirit. "Or do you not know that your body is the temple of the Holy Spirit who is in you, whom you have from God, and you are not your own? For you were bought at a price; therefore glorify God in your body and in your spirit, which are God's" (1 Corinthians 6:19–20).

We live in a high-tech/no-touch world where people are increasingly "loners." Jesus predicted this would happen. He said, "And because lawlessness will abound, the love of many will grow cold" (Matthew 24:12). Yet this cannot be the lifestyle of fervent Christians. We are not allowed the seeming luxury of sealing ourselves away from each other. We need each other. In the Church, we strive for that "unity of the faith and of the knowledge of the Son of God, to a perfect man, to the measure of the stature of the fullness of Christ; that we should no longer be children, tossed to and fro and carried about with every wind of doctrine, by the trickery of men, in the cunning craftiness of deceitful plotting, but, speaking the truth in love, may grow up in all things into Him who is the head — Christ — from whom the whole body, joined and knit together by what every joint supplies, according to the effective working by which every part does its share, causes growth of the body for the edifying of itself in love" (Ephesians 4:13–16).

Are you doing your share as part of the body of Christ? It is impossible to sustain a strong love and witness for the Lord without the love and support of His people. Just as one log may burn for a little while, when many logs are put together, they draw warmth from each other and burn even brighter.

The Privilege of Giving

Why should you go to church anyway? To hear the music? To hear the pastor preach? What's the purpose of meeting together?

The primary purpose of meeting corporately is to give, not to get. True, you will receive blessings from this experience but that is not the main reason for being a strong, fellowshiping member. Jesus said, "Give, and it will be given to you: good measure, pressed down, shaken together, and running over will be put into your bosom. For with the same measure that you use, it will be measured back to you" (Luke 6:38). The purpose of meeting is giving.

First, you give to the Lord. The Psalmist said, "Give unto the LORD, O you mighty ones, give unto the LORD glory and strength. Give unto the LORD the glory due to His name; Worship the LORD in the beauty of holiness" (Psalm 29:1–2). You give to the Lord as you praise His name and worship Him. A heart of joyful praise should be the trademark of every Christian. In fact, when the Holy Spirit fills your life, you will be "speaking to one another in psalms and hymns and spiritual songs, singing and making melody in your heart to the Lord, giving thanks always for all things to God the Father in the name of our Lord Jesus Christ, submitting to one another in the fear of God" (Ephesians 5:19–21).

But you also give to the Lord by giving of your finances to His cause through the Church. The Bible commands us, " 'Bring all the tithes into the storehouse, that there may be food in My house, and try Me now in this,' says the LORD of hosts, 'if I will not open for you the windows of heaven and pour out for you such blessing that there will not be room enough to receive it' " (Malachi 3:10).

The tithe is one-tenth of your income. The Bible says it belongs to God. Above the tithe, God may speak to your heart to give Him a financial offering of praise for His goodness to you. Also, He will impress you at times to give alms gifts to the poor and to assist His worldwide missions enterprise. One of the greatest joys in life is to give of your finances, knowing that God will bless you even more. "And God is able to make all grace abound toward you, that you, always having all sufficiency in all things, may have an abundance for every good work" (2 Corinthians 9:8).

Yes, your privilege and responsibility as part of His church is to give to the Lord both your worship and finances. In fact, giving your finances is a token of giving yourself, for your money is what you have in exchange for time you have spent in work. The Psalmist said, "What shall I render to the Lord for all His benefits toward me? I will take up the cup of salvation, and call upon the name of the Lord. I will pay my vows to the Lord now in the presence of all His people" (Psalm 116:12–14).

When the Church meets, not only do you give to the Lord, you also give to His people — your brothers and sisters in Christ. The closer we get to the return of Christ to earth, so much more are we to encourage each other by meeting together publicly to worship the Lord and be instructed in our walk with Him. "And let us consider one another in order to stir up love and good works, not forsaking the assembling of ourselves together, as is the manner of some, but exhorting one another, and so much the more as you see the Day approaching" (Hebrews 10:24–25).

Now you are enabled to give to the world — to those who so desperately need what we have found in Jesus Christ. Having been nurtured by worship, exhortation from the Word and fellowship with other believers in Christ, you are ready to share the love of Jesus with those who have not yet come to know Him.

What Kind of Church?

When I speak on the importance of the Church, I am often asked, "What kind of church should I attend? After all, there are so many denominations and so many types of churches. Which one is the right one?" Of course, this is a very complex question. Our God is a God of variety. Certain churches seem better suited for some people than others. However, in any church where you identify, there should be at least three distinguishing marks.

First, you should unite with a church where *Jesus Christ is central in all that is said and done.* Unfortunately, this is not the case in every church. There are churches whose chief identity is their own pet minor doctrine. Don't get caught up in any church that is not first and foremost a Jesus church. Paul said, "For I determined not to know anything among you except Jesus Christ and Him crucified" (1 Corinthians 2:2). Any deviation from the central theme of Jesus Christ should be a danger signal, warning you to keep clear.

Second, you should unite with a church where *the Bible is preached as the authoritative Word of God.* Steer away from any group that claims to have "further written revelation" apart from the Bible. Find a church where the Bible is honored as God's love letter to man, truth without any mixture of error.

Finally, you should unite with a church where you will be *free to worship the Lord in spirit and in truth.* We are living in a wonderful time when God is restoring the gifts and power of the Holy Spirit to His church. Look for a church that honors the work of the Holy Spirit and allows Him to move freely when they meet together.

Other than your Lord, perhaps your most valuable possessions are your brothers and sisters in Christ. You need them. They need you. So, unite with a strong church where Jesus is preached and worshiped as Lord. And don't wait. Do it now.

TAKE A STEP OF ACTION!

❏ I have united with a Christ-exalting church and I am regularly fellowshiping there with my brothers and sisters in Christ.

❏ Remember: "And let us consider one another in order to stir up love and good works, not forsaking the assembling of ourselves together, as is the manner of some, but exhorting one another, and so much the more as you see the Day approaching" (Hebrews 10:24–25).

STEP SIX

Lay the Proper Foundations

In Psalm 11:3, the piercing question is asked, "If the foundations are destroyed, what can the righteous do?" In this day when people appear to be severed from their roots, a proper foundation is more vital than ever.

Years ago, our family built a new home. It seemed that a very long time elapsed as the ground was leveled, piers were poured, and the foundation laid according to exacting standards. Then the structure of the house seemed to go up quickly. The foundation had taken a long time to set, yet nothing could have been built without it. The devil knows that without a strong foundation, no matter how impressive your Christian "house" may look, it is destined to collapse. That is why he does his utmost to keep you from laying an adequate foundation. In this "instant" age, we seem to loathe anything that takes time. Yet if you do not take the time now to lay a proper foundation, you will have to come back years later, perhaps having to tear down everything that was built, to set a solid foundation.

Of course, the foundation for every Christian is Jesus himself. "For no other foundation can anyone lay than that which is laid, which is Jesus Christ" (1 Corinthians 3:11). Jesus urges us to build on the firm foundation of an abiding relationship with Him. This will steady us against all of life's storms. "Therefore whoever hears these sayings of Mine, and does them, I will liken him to a wise man who built his house on the rock: and the rain descended, the floods came, and the winds blew and beat on that house; and it did not fall, for it was founded on the rock" (Matthew 7:24–25).

Also, there are basic foundational principles of right thinking and living that must be laid properly if your life in Christ is to be fruitful. The writer of Hebrews said that we are to put these foundation principles in place at the beginning of our life-long walk with the Lord, so that we can move on toward maturity in Christ. "Therefore, leaving the discussion of the elementary principles of Christ, let us go on to perfection, not laying again the foundation of repentance from dead works and of faith toward God, of the doctrine of baptisms, of laying on of hands, of resurrection of the dead, and of eternal judgment" (Hebrews 6:1–2). Let's look at each of these elementary principles which make up the foundation.

Repentance from Dead Works

Someone has well said, "God only saves *repentant* sinners." There is no such thing as salvation without repentance. The call to repent — to turn from sin — was the first word of John the Baptist, Jesus, and His disciples. Jesus said, "Unless you repent you will all likewise perish" (Luke 13:5). We come to God initially by repentance. We continue to get closer to the Lord by a lifestyle of repentance; a continual turning from sin to God.

Repentance is not only a turning *from*, it is also a turning *to*. One repents from sin and turns to God, exercising faith in the Lord Jesus Christ. You experience "repentance toward God and faith toward our Lord Jesus Christ" (Acts 20:21).

But notice, repentance is not only from sin. It is also "repentance from dead works." In other words, you must repent or turn from the idea that your good works could ever merit salvation. You must forever turn from the idea that your good works (the Bible calls them "dead works") could ever be your ticket to heaven. To become a true Christian, you must turn from your sins — and even from your own goodness — to trust in Jesus Christ alone for your salvation. "For by grace [God's unmerited favor] you have been saved through faith, and that not of yourselves; it is the gift of God, not of works, lest anyone should boast" (Ephesians 2:8–9). "Not by works of righteousness which we have done, but according to His mercy He saved us, through the washing of regeneration and renewing of the Holy Spirit" (Titus 3:5).

Faith toward God

Faith toward God is the flip side of the coin of repentance from dead works. You stop trusting in yourself and start trusting in God for your salvation. But not only are you to trust the Lord to save you, you are to trust Him for everything else as well. The Bible says, "As you have therefore received Christ Jesus the Lord, so walk in Him" (Colossians 2:6). How did you receive Christ? By faith. How are you to walk in Him? The same way — by faith. What is faith? "Now faith is the substance of things hoped for, the evidence of things not seen" (Hebrews 11:1).

God responds to faith. It is one of the three abiding character-istics of true Christian living — faith, hope, and love. "But without faith it is impossible to please Him, for he who comes to God must believe that He is, and that He is a rewarder of those who diligently seek Him" (Hebrews 11:6). In a day of skepticism and unbelief, your faith will bring great rewards in your walk with the Lord.

The Doctrine of Baptisms

There are at least three baptisms spoken of in the Bible. First, there is that baptism whereby you are *baptized into Christ.* This happens the moment you are born again. "For by one Spirit we were all baptized into one body — whether Jews or Greeks, whether slave or free — and have all been made to drink into one Spirit" (1 Corinthians 12:13).

Second, there is *water baptism* for the believer in Jesus Christ. If you, as a Christian, have not yet been baptized in water, go back immediately and re-read Step Two. Then, prepare to follow Christ in water baptism at the earliest opportunity.

Third, there is the *baptism with the Holy Spirit.* Jesus said, "John truly baptized with water, but you shall be baptized with the Holy Spirit not many days from now" (Acts 1:5). If you have not yet received the baptism with the Holy Spirit, re-read Step Three. Then ask God in faith to fill you with His Spirit.

Are you a genuine follower of Christ, trusting only in Him for salvation? If so, you have been baptized into Christ. As a Christian, have you been baptized in water? Then, have you been baptized in the Holy Spirit? Don't fail to lay these vital parts of the foundation.

Laying on of Hands

To some Christians, this may seem an obscure doctrine to be placed in the essentials of a good foundation. But remember that many of the major events of the Bible happened in conjunction with the laying on of hands. Jesus laid His hands on the sick and healed them. The apostles laid their hands on believers and they were filled with the Holy Spirit. The elders laid their hands upon ministers and they received gifts of the Spirit. Early church leaders laid their hands on missionaries and sent them out in service. Jesus laid His hands on children and blessed them.

Now that you are His, and now that you have allowed the Holy Spirit to fill you, your hands can become an extension of the touch of Jesus, bringing healing, power, and blessing. As you literally touch those around you with the compassion of Jesus, His power will flow through you. One man said it like this: "Put your heart in your hands."

Resurrection of the Dead

Jesus promised, "I am the resurrection and the life. He who believes in Me, though he may die, he shall live" (John 11:25). He went on to say, "Because I live, you will live also" (John 14:19). The central theme of the gospel is the death, burial, and bodily resurrection of Jesus Christ. Now you can know that one glorious day, He will resurrect all those now dead who have put their trust in Jesus. "But now Christ is risen from the dead, and has become the firstfruits of those who have fallen asleep" (1 Corinthians 15:20).

When a Christian's body ceases functioning, only his body dies. The real inner person immediately is transported into the presence of the Lord in heaven. The Bible comforts us by assuring us that to be absent from the body is to be present with the Lord (see 2 Corinthians 5:8). When Jesus returns, the resurrected bodies of all Christians will be reunited with their spirits, already departed. "For the Lord Himself will descend from heaven with a shout, with the voice of an archangel, and with the trumpet of God. And the dead in Christ will rise first. Then we who are alive and remain shall be caught up together with them in the clouds to meet the Lord in the air. And thus we shall always be with the Lord" (1 Thessalonians 4:16-17).

Don't be victimized by a temporal style of Christianity that robs you of the blessed hope of Jesus' return and your future with Him. Enjoy your present walk with the Lord and look forward to your future — forever with the Lord!

Eternal Judgment

When Jesus comes again to earth, He will come to judge the world for sin and unbelief. Jesus has saved you, however, from this terrible coming wrath because you belong to Him. Now that you are His, you are to "serve the living and true God, and to wait for His Son from heaven, whom He raised from the dead, even Jesus who delivers us from the wrath to come" (1 Thessalonians 1:9–10). When Jesus returns, He will come "in flaming fire taking vengeance on those who do not know God, and on those who do not obey the gospel of our Lord Jesus Christ. These shall be punished with everlasting destruction from the presence of the Lord and from the glory of His power" (2 Thessalonians 1:8–9).

In light of this coming cosmic judgment, Peter reminds us, "Therefore, since all these things will be dissolved, what manner of persons ought you to be in holy conduct and godliness, looking for and hastening the coming of the day of God, because of which the heavens will be dissolved, being on fire, and the elements will melt with fervent heat?" (2 Peter 3:11–12).

Thank God, as a true believer in Jesus Christ, you will never stand in judgment for your sins. Jesus took the judgment you deserved when He died for you on the cross. But you will give an account of your post-conversion life to the Lord. Paul said, "For we must all appear before the judgment seat of Christ, that each one may receive the things done in the body, according to what he has done, whether good or bad" (2 Corinthians 5:10). Just think of it! One day you will stand and give an account of your life before Jesus. If you receive His "well done," then your life will have been a success (see Matthew 25:21).

Start now by laying a strong foundation. Remember what Jesus said: "Whoever comes to Me, and hears My sayings and does them, I will show you whom he is like: He is like a man building a house, who dug deep and laid the foundation on the rock. And when the flood arose, the stream beat vehemently against that house, and could not shake it, for it was founded on the rock" (Luke 6:47–48).

Lay your foundation in the rock, Christ Jesus.

TAKE A STEP OF ACTION!

❒ I have laid the proper foundation on which to build my life in Christ.

❒ Remember: "As you have therefore received Christ Jesus the Lord, so walk in Him, rooted and built up in Him and established in the faith, as you have been taught, abounding in it with thanksgiving" (Colossians 2:6–7).

STEP SEVEN

Let the Bible Speak to You

A sophisticated Westerner on vacation saw a man from a remote Pacific island sitting under a tree, reading his Bible. "Don't you know that's an antiquated myth?" the Westerner laughed. Looking up, the islander calmly smiled and replied, "Sir, some years ago this book was brought to this island. If you had arrived before this book, I would be having you tonight for dinner — literally."

No book in history has influenced lives and nations as has the Bible. George Washington said, "It is impossible rightly to govern without God and the Bible." Our nation's ethics and morality are based on the Bible. Our laws stem from the Bible.

Not only is the Bible the standard for society, but it is especially the standard by which Christians are to live. "All Scripture is given by inspiration of God, and is profitable for doctrine, for reproof, for correction, for instruction in righteousness, that the man of God may be complete, thoroughly equipped for every good work" (2 Timothy 3:16–17). In the original language, this verse begins, "All Scripture is God-breathed. . . ." As the very breathed-out Word of God, we are to heed what the Bible says. We are not to judge the Bible. We are to allow the Bible to judge us. The Bible is God's love letter to you. Through its sacred pages God speaks to you — guiding, warning, correcting, and expressing His love.

What the Bible Is All About

The Bible is comprised of 66 books written by some 40 authors over a span of some 1,600 years. Its divine author is the Holy Spirit. "Knowing this first, that no prophecy of Scripture is of any private interpretation, for prophecy never came by the will of man, but holy men of God spoke as they were moved by the Holy Spirit" (2 Peter 1:20–21). The great English preacher of the 19th century, Charles Spurgeon, said, "The Book is a divine production; it is perfect, and is the last court of appeal — 'the judge which ends all strife.' I would as soon dream of blaspheming my Maker as of questioning the infallibility of His Word."

The central theme of the Bible is redemption — the love story of God bringing broken people back to himself. You will see through its pages a scarlet thread of redemption as God goes to incredible lengths, even to the sending of His Son to die, so that you and I can be redeemed and brought back to Him.

The Bible is divided into two sections: the Old Testament and the New Testament. In the Old Testament, the Law and the Prophets pointed to the coming Redeemer who would be sacrificed for humanity's sinful rebellion. In the New Testament, Jesus of Nazareth is revealed as God's Son, His agent of redemption, who will one day rule the earth as King of kings and Lord of lords.

The first five books of the Bible, Genesis through Deuteronomy, are often called the *Books of the Law*. They tell how God created the world, revealed His will by giving the Ten Commandments, and called the children of Israel to be a light to show the one true God to all people.

The *Books of History*, Joshua through Esther, chronicle Israel's intermittent disobedience and repentance and God's steadfast love toward them.

The *Books of Poetry*, Job through the Song of Solomon, run the gamut of human emotions, showing us God's presence with us both in times of exhilaration and in times of despair.

The *Books of the Prophets*, Isaiah through Malachi, record God's prophetic warnings, judgment, and tender love toward His people.

The Old Testament is of tremendous value to us today as Christians. In the Old Testament, we see God's plan of redemption progressively being revealed until it would one day be climaxed as God's Son hung bleeding on a Roman cross. Regarding the Old Testament Scriptures, Paul reminds us, "For whatever things were written before were written for our learning, that we through the patience and comfort of the Scriptures might have hope" (Rom. 15:4).

In the New Testament, God reveals His new covenant based on the sacrifice of His Son for humanity's sin. *The Gospels*, Matthew through John, are error-free, biographical accounts of the life and ministry of Jesus.

The Book of Acts is the historical account of the life of the early church. This book is also the pattern for church life today.

The letters to the churches and individuals, Romans through Jude, define Christian doctrine and practical living for us today.

The Book of the Revelation is a prophetic look into the future when the earth ultimately comes under the full rule of Jesus Christ.

How to Study the Bible

In every book, in every line of Scripture, God desires to speak to you. As you open your Bible, pray that God will open your eyes to His truth for you. Let your prayer be, "Open my eyes, that I may see wondrous things from Your law" (Psalm 119:18). The line of a great hymn says, "Beyond the sacred page, I seek Thee, Lord." Ask the Lord to reveal himself to you through His Word.

So come reverently to the Bible, and come expectantly. You should expect God to speak to you because this is a living Book. "For the word of God is living and powerful, and sharper than any two-edged sword, piercing even to the division of soul and spirit, and of joints and marrow, and is a discerner of the thoughts and intents of the heart" (Hebrews 4:12).

As you meditate on Scripture and obey its truths, God promises to crown your life with success. "This Book of the Law shall not depart from your mouth, but you shall meditate in it day and night, that you may observe to do according to all that is written in it. For then you will make your way prosperous, and then you will have good success" (Joshua 1:8).

How to Start

Begin by reading the Gospel of John. As you read, throw away all your preconceptions of Jesus and allow the Holy Spirit to reveal Him to you in a fresh way. You may wish to supplement your reading of John with other portions of Scripture. For instance, if you read five Psalms and one chapter from Proverbs each day, you will complete the Books of Psalms and Proverbs in one month. After a year of daily meditation in Psalms and Proverbs, just watch how your life will begin to change.

After you have read and studied the Gospel of John, read the Book of Romans. It is the clearest and most definitive presentation of the gospel in the Bible. Perhaps you would want to take one book of the Bible as your life-project, memorizing the entire book and devouring each truth from its pages.

As you study, keep in mind that a quiet place is a real help. Many people find that the early morning hours are excellent for Bible reading. Others find the lunch hour or the evening better. Whatever is best for you, remember to be meditating on the Bible's truths both "day and night."

Also, keep in mind that a good modern version of the Bible will help you comprehend its truths. In fact, an excellent way to study the Bible is to compare two or three versions as you read.

Don't forget Scripture memory. Some hostages and prisoners of war who were later released have said that their knowledge of God's Word was their most precious asset during their difficult ordeal. In your life as well, nothing could be more valuable than your knowledge of the Word of God — and your intimate knowledge of the God of the Word. Begin by memorizing the key verses at the end of each chapter of this book.

Look around you. Everything you see is in the process of wearing away. Everything, that is, except the Word of God. "The grass withers, the flower fades, but the word of our God stands forever" (Isaiah 40:8).

TAKE A STEP OF ACTION!

❏ I am reading and studying the Bible daily.

❏ Remember: "Your word is a lamp to my feet and a light to my path" (Psalm 119:105).

STEP EIGHT

Talk to God in Prayer

If tomorrow the president requested to see you at the White House, you would spare no expense to meet his request. At any cost, you would make that important appointment. Why? Because a man of great authority desired to talk to you. Yet the God of the universe, the King above all kings and the Lord above all lords, desires to talk to you! Are you making that appointment? God has invited you to commune with Him.

Prayer is communion with God. In prayer, you speak to God about yourself and you speak to God concerning others. There could be no higher privilege on earth than to be ushered into the throne-room of the God of the universe. Because of the blood of Jesus, you and I have this direct access to God anytime, anywhere. "Therefore, brethren, having boldness to enter the Holiest by the blood of Jesus, by a new and living way which He consecrated for us, through the veil, that is, His flesh, and having a High Priest over the house of God, let us draw near with a true heart in full assurance of faith, having our hearts sprinkled from an evil conscience and our bodies washed with pure water" (Hebrews 10:19–22).

Your Hotline to Heaven

Imagine the possibility of helping shape the course of human history by your prayers. Yes, you have the opportunity to literally change the world by bringing God's will into effect through prayer. Your own life will be changed by prayer. The lives of your loved ones will be changed and even entire nations can be affected by your prayers.

God gave an incredible promise to those who will be serious concerning this matter of prayer. He said, "Call to Me, and I will answer you, and show you great and mighty things, which you do not know" (Jeremiah 33:3). Are you desiring to see "great and mighty things"? They can be yours as you pray.

You literally have a hotline to heaven. Because of the new and living way which Jesus opened for every Christian by His blood, you have direct access to God.

I will never forget standing on the balcony of my hotel room in a distant country. In those early morning hours I listened to the cries of sincere religious people as they chanted their prayers. Yet few, if any, of these people would ever hope in their wildest dreams to actually have the privilege of communing with God. But that is your birthright as a believer in Jesus Christ.

We are to pray for several reasons. For one thing, God urges us to pray. Also, so much good is accomplished through prayer. Alfred, Lord Tennyson was right: "More things are wrought through prayer than this world dreams of."

This very moment you, as a Christian, have a privilege only dreamed of by those in former ages. You have direct access to God because of Jesus' blood. By this "new and living way," you can enter directly into God's presence.

When you pray, it is not necessary to use religious-sounding words. In fact, Jesus denounced those who made a show of their prayers and thought that they would be heard "for their many words" (Matthew 6:7–8.) Instead of religious oratory, Jesus urged simple, sincere prayer to God, even encouraging us to call the Almighty God "our Father" (Matthew 6:9).

The Lord Jesus offers us spectacular promises of answered prayer when we come to Him in faith using the authority of His name. He said, "And whatever you ask in My name, that I will do, that the Father may be glorified in the Son. If you ask anything in My name, I will do it" (John 14:13–14). Just think of it! The power of heaven is at your disposal as you pray in Jesus' name!

How to Pray

In what attitude should you pray? First, pray *committedly*. In other words, you should have a set time for prayer as well as carrying a spirit of worship and prayer throughout the day. Remember that Peter and John went up together to the temple at a set hour of prayer (see Acts 3:1).

Second, pray *fervently*. It is those who are fervent in prayer who press into kingdom possibilities. "The effective, fervent prayer of a righteous man avails much" (James 5:16).

Third, pray *specifically*. Are there family members and friends you want to see come to faith in Christ? They can come to Christ — and will — as you pray in faith. Did you ever stop to think that you can wield a scepter of life or death by your prayers?

Jesus gave a colossal promise, "And I will give you the keys of the kingdom of heaven, and whatever you bind on earth will be bound in heaven, and whatever you loose on earth will be loosed in heaven" (Matthew 16:19).

Fourth, pray *unitedly*. This was one of the great keys to the effectiveness of the early church. When confronted with persecution, they raised their voice to God with one accord (Acts 4:24).

Fifth, pray *persistently*. Jesus taught that persistence in prayer will yield results. "So I say to you, ask, and it will be given to you; seek, and you will find; knock, and it will be opened to you" (Luke 11:9).

Sixth, pray *boldly*. "Let us therefore come boldly to the throne of grace, that we may obtain mercy and find grace to help in time of need" (Hebrews 4:16).

Finally, pray *expectantly*. "Now this is the confidence that we have in Him, that if we ask anything according to His will, He hears us. And if we know that He hears us, whatever we ask, we know that we have the petitions that we have asked of Him" (1 John 5:14–15).

In answer to the disciples' request, "Lord, teach us to pray," Jesus provided for them a model prayer. Each phrase of this prayer can be a prompting to further prayer.

> Our Father in heaven,
> Hallowed be Your name.
> Your kingdom come.
> Your will be done
> On earth as it is in heaven.
> Give us this day our daily bread.
> And forgive us our debts,

As we forgive our debtors.
And do not lead us into temptation,
But deliver us from the evil one.
For Yours is the kingdom and the
Power and the glory forever. Amen
(Matthew 6:9–13).

Let this model prayer of Jesus be your springboard to loving communication with God.

The Theater of War

In Ephesians 6, Paul reminds us that we are living in a state of war against the devil. Because of this he urges us, "Put on the whole armor of God, that you may be able to stand against the wiles of the devil. . . . Stand therefore, having girded your waist with truth, having put on the breastplate of righteousness, and having shod your feet with the preparation of the gospel of peace; above all, taking the shield of faith with which you will be able to quench all the fiery darts of the wicked one. And take the helmet of salvation, and the sword of the Spirit, which is the word of God" (Ephesians 6:11–17).

Begin each day by mentally putting on this spiritual armor. In so doing you are simply putting on different aspects of the life of the Lord Jesus. "But put on the Lord Jesus Christ, and make no provision for the flesh, to fulfill its lusts" (Romans 13:14).

After you have spiritually "suited up" for battle, where then is the arena of war? Paul gives the answer to that question in Ephesians 6:18. After urging the Christian to put on this elaborate armor, he then urges him to be "praying always with all prayer and supplication in the Spirit, being watchful to this end with all perseverance and supplication for all the saints." In other words, after we have put on the Lord Jesus, we then go to war against the devil. The primary arena of our battle against him and his forces is the arena of prayer, for it is there that Satan's forces are defeated and the Christian wins the victory. Have you suited up for the war? If so, are you going into battle?

Begin Now

There is no better time to begin this life of dynamic praying than today. Begin now by using the model prayer that Jesus gave in Matthew 6:9–13. Let every phrase of this prayer be the springboard for you to open your heart to God.

Set a specific place for prayer. Jesus departed to "the place of prayer." Set a specific time for concerted prayer. Peter and John went to the temple at "the hour of prayer." So set a consistent time and place to get before the Lord.

As you pray, believe God for answers. Jesus assured us, "Therefore I say to you, whatever things you ask when you pray, believe that you receive them, and you will have them" (Mark 11:24).

God is wonderfully diverse in the types of people He uses. However, those whom He uses have one thing in common. All of them have learned the power of prayer. You can be a world-changer. Let it begin now. In humility, yet in boldness because of the blood of Jesus, approach your Father in His heavenly throne room.

TAKE A STEP OF ACTION!

❏ I am developing an intimate relationship with God through prayer.

❏ Remember: "Call to Me, and I will answer you, and show you great and mighty things, which you do not know" (Jeremiah 33:3).

STEP NINE

Reach Others
for Jesus

There is no greater honor in life than sharing your faith in Christ with others. Jesus has bequeathed to you His own power for this task. He promised, "But you shall receive power when the Holy Spirit has come upon you; and you shall be witnesses to Me in Jerusalem, and in all Judea and Samaria, and to the end of the earth" (Acts 1:8). He has commanded us to extend our witness for Him to the very extremities of the earth. "Go into all the world and preach the gospel to every creature" (Mark 16:15).

Not only is it your privilege to share the good news of Christ, it is your responsibility. God commands us to warn the wicked to turn from their ways. "When I say to the wicked, 'You shall surely die,' and you give him no warning, nor speak to warn the wicked from his wicked way, to save his life, that same wicked man shall die in his iniquity; but his blood I will require at your hand. Yet, if you warn the wicked, and he does not turn from his wickedness, nor from his wicked way, he shall die in his iniquity; but you have delivered your soul" (Ezekiel 3:18–19).

Imagine that you had discovered the cure for cancer. How cruel and uncaring it would be to keep the cure hidden from those who so desperately need it. Yet you and I have found the cure for sin — a living relationship with Jesus Christ as Savior and Lord. The world has been infested with sin. We have been invested with the cure.

The World Only You Can Reach

You are the only "Bible" that many people will ever read. Because you are a Christian, whether you like it or not, people are "reading" your life. As they look at you, what do they see? What is the life message you are portraying?

The apostle Paul said, "For none of us lives to himself and no one dies to himself" (Romans 14:7). Your life is affecting the lives of others. Even the least influential person directly affects the lives of others.

You live in concentric circles of relationships with your family, relatives, friends, school or business acquaintances, and others whom you meet. In every relationship, you should be concerned to conduct yourself as a worthy ambassador of Jesus Christ. "Now then, we are ambassadors for Christ, as though God were pleading through us: we implore you on Christ's behalf, be reconciled to God" (2 Corinthians 5:20). Remember that your life is pointing people in some direction. Are you pointing them to Jesus?

Are You Qualified?

What are the qualifications to be an effective witness for Jesus Christ?

First, of course, you must have experienced a genuine conversion yourself. You cannot impart what you do not possess. Jesus said, "Out of the abundance of the heart the mouth speaks" (Matthew 12:34). If your heart is filled with Jesus, your mouth will be filled with the message about Him.

Second, you must have an assurance of your own salvation. In Step One of this book we dealt at some length with this topic. If there is any doubt in your heart at all concerning your relationship with Jesus Christ, I encourage you to read again "Your Most Important Step" and Step One. You see, if you are unsure of your own relationship with the Lord, it will be very difficult to share with certainty that relationship with others. So I urge you to settle the question of your assurance of salvation.

Third, to be an effective witness for Christ, you must allow the Holy Spirit to control your life. During the dynamic days of growth of the first century church, multiplied thousands were added to the Lord. This was in direct answer to the prayers of those early Christians for boldness to witness for Christ. After they had prayed for boldness, the Bible says that "the place where they were assembled together was shaken; and they were all filled with the Holy Spirit, and they spoke the word of God with boldness" (Acts 4:31). You too will experience boldness as you allow the Spirit of God to control your life. If you are in the presence of Jesus, it will be evident to those around you, just as it was obvious to those who saw the lives of Peter and John. "Now when they saw the boldness of Peter and John, and perceived that they were uneducated and untrained men, they marveled. And they realized that they had been with Jesus" (Acts 4:13).

Finally, you must have a love and compassion for people. As you share your faith in Christ, it will be clear to those around you if you genuinely love them. When the devil does not seemingly give way to prayer, he does give way to prayer coupled with tears. "Those who sow in tears shall reap in joy. He who continually goes forth weeping, bearing seed for sowing, shall doubtless come again with rejoicing, bringing his sheaves with him" (Psalm 126:5–6). God places His love for people in our hearts by the Holy Spirit. (Read Romans 5:5; Galatians 5:22.)

Breaking the Silence Barrier

Why is it that we seem capable of talking about every subject under heaven except *the subject of heaven* — salvation through Jesus Christ? Sometimes it seems difficult to turn a conversation to spiritual matters. Allow me to make a few suggestions on how you can begin in sharing your faith in Christ with others.

First, share your testimony of how you came to know Christ. You might begin by saying something like this: "May I share with you the most wonderful thing that ever happened to me?" Then proceed to tell the person exactly how you came into a living relationship with Christ. After you have shared your testimony with him, simply ask, "Has this ever happened to you?"

Another way to begin sharing the gospel is to ask, "Have you ever made the wonderful discovery of knowing Jesus Christ personally?" If the person answers negatively, respond by saying, "You would like to, wouldn't you?" Then share with him the good news of how Jesus Christ died on the cross for his sins, rose again from the dead, and offers new life to him right now.

Still another way to share the love of Christ is to inform the person with whom you are talking about the wonderful things God is doing in your church. If Jesus is manifesting His presence in the congregation, people will want to come experience His life. When Jesus came to Capernaum, "It was heard that He was in the house. Immediately many gathered together, so that there was no longer room to receive them, not even near the door" (Mark 2:1–2). When you share that "Jesus is in the house," people will want to come and see what the Lord is doing in your church family.

I have made it a rule of my life that I will not talk to anyone more than ten minutes without letting them know that I love the Lord Jesus with all my heart. As you walk in communion with the Lord, the natural outflow of His life in you will be His life through you and His message on your lips.

Becoming a World Christian

As has already been stated, no one lives in a vacuum. Because of advances in communications and technology, our world is now a global village. What happens to starving children, victimized women, or persecuted Christians in distant lands affects you. You have a responsibility to your world.

When Jesus commissioned His disciples to spread His message, the only limit that He put on the advance of the gospel was "to the end of the earth" (see Acts 1:8). We should not rest until every person has had the opportunity to hear the message of Jesus Christ presented in an intelligent, Holy Spirit-anointed way, and accept it.

David Livingstone, the great British missionary to Africa, said, "God had an only Son and He was a missionary." Have you desired high and holy purpose for your life? There could be no more thrilling and fulfilling purpose than to advance the gospel of Jesus Christ, especially among those who have never heard.

How can you help the cause of Christ worldwide? First, by praying. Jesus said, "The harvest truly is plentiful, but the laborers are few. Therefore pray the Lord of the harvest to send out laborers into His harvest" (Matthew 9:37–38). After you pray that God will grant massive, global harvest with millions being added to the family of God, then be willing to be the answer to your own prayer for more laborers.

Second, you can help the cause of world evangelization by giving. Someone has well said, "The gospel is free but it takes money to pipe it to the ends of the earth." I believe God will allow many people reading this book to accumulate great wealth, not so they may consume it themselves, but so their wealth can be used to spread the gospel. As God blesses you financially, remember your responsibility to a needy world.

Third, you can help the cause of missions by going. Perhaps God has not called you to be a vocational missionary. Then again, perhaps He has. Only you can settle that issue before the Lord. However, there are a number of other options. For instance, you could take your vacation in another nation and share your faith wherever you go. Or you may wish to consider a short-term mission trip. You may prayerfully consider asking your company to transfer you to an overseas assignment. While there, you can strengthen the churches and Christians of that area and share the gospel with those who do not know Christ.

Jesus Christ has given you the unspeakable privilege of representing Him in the world today. There could be no higher calling. Now, by the power of God's indwelling Spirit, live a life that will bring honor to the Christ you love and the gospel you share. As Paul said, "I, therefore, the prisoner of the Lord, beseech you to walk worthy of the calling with which you were called, with all lowliness and gentleness, with long-suffering, bearing with one another in love, endeavoring to keep the unity of the Spirit in the bond of peace" (Ephesians 4:1–3).

TAKE A STEP OF ACTION!

❏ I am sharing my faith in Jesus Christ with others.

❏ Remember: "But you shall receive power when the Holy Spirit has come upon you; and you shall be witnesses to Me in Jerusalem, and in all Judea and Samaria, and to the end of the earth" (Acts 1:8).

STEP TEN

Trust God's Promises

As this book comes to a close, I could give you no better advice than to trust the promises of God. You can be certain of this: You have come into contact with a trustworthy God. The Bible says that God simply cannot lie. Therefore, you can trust Him implicitly in every circumstance of life.

Because God is trustworthy, His promises to you can be trusted. He will not fail. He cannot fail you. It is impossible for God to lie. It is also impossible for God to fail.

The promises that God has given to you in the Bible are magnificent. It is by laying hold of these promises that you come to know God better and actually partake in His life. Peter greeted his fellow-believers, "Grace and peace be multiplied to you in the knowledge of God and of Jesus our Lord, as His divine power has given to us all things that pertain to life and godliness, through the knowledge of Him who called us by glory and virtue, by which have been given to us exceedingly great and precious promises, that through these you may be partakers of the divine nature, having escaped the corruption that is in the world through lust" (2 Peter 1:2–4).

Do you see what these verses say? Peter says that through the "exceedingly great and precious promises" that God has given to you, you come to know Him better and literally share in His life. Therefore, it is important for you to know the promises of God and to hold them as your own.

The Promise of His Presence

Jesus promised, "I will never leave you nor forsake you" (Hebrews 13:5). What more wonderful promise could there be? Here lies the basis for your acceptance before God: Jesus has promised never to leave you.

But not only has He promised to be with you throughout life, He has promised to manifest His presence to you as you praise Him and worship Him. The Bible says that God dwells in the praises of His people. "But You are holy, enthroned in the praises of Israel" (Psalm 22:3). As you learn to praise Him both personally and corporately with your church family, you will experience His powerful presence.

When you know that the Lord is with you, all of life has a thread of joy running through it. "You will show me the path of life; in Your presence is fullness of joy; at Your right hand are pleasures forevermore" (Psalm 16:11). And even during the dark hours of your life the Lord has promised that He will not leave you. David said, "Yea, though I walk through the valley of the shadow of death, I will fear no evil; for You are with me . . ." (Psalm 23:4).

So trust His promise to you — the promise of His presence.

The Promise of His Purpose

For the Christian, nothing happens by accident. Every occurrence of your life is purposeful and with design. God is doing something in you. He has an over-arching purpose for your life. What is it? God's purpose for you is to conform you into the image of the Lord Jesus Christ.

To accomplish this, God uses the circumstances of life, thus molding you and producing in you the character of Jesus. That is why you can echo with the apostle Paul, "And we know that all things work together for good to those who love God, to those who are the called according to His purpose. For whom He foreknew, He also predestined to be conformed to the image of His Son, that He might be the firstborn among many brethren" (Romans 8:28–29). This passage assures you that God will engineer the circumstances of your life, even those that the devil means for ill against you, to make you more Christ-like. There is no doubt that God will succeed in this overall purpose. Nothing in earth or hell can deter His plan for you. "Being confident of this very thing, that He who has begun a good work in you will complete it until the day of Jesus Christ" (Philippians 1:6). So trust the promise of His purpose.

The Promise of His Provision

Even from the time of Abraham, God has revealed himself as the Lord who provides (see Genesis 22:14). Do not look to any human as your primary source of provision. God is your source. He will provide all your needs. He will provide for you physically. He will provide for you financially. He will provide for you emotionally. He will certainly provide for you spiritually. "And my God shall supply all your need according to His riches in glory by Christ Jesus" (Philippians 4:19).

The treasury of heaven is full. The resources of heaven will never be bankrupt. You can draw upon God's provision in Christ Jesus for all your needs.

The Promise of His Power

Just before His ascension into heaven, Jesus assured His disciples, "All authority has been given to me in heaven and on earth. Go therefore and make disciples of all the nations, baptizing them in the name of the Father and of the Son and of the Holy Spirit, teaching them to observe all things that I have commanded you; and lo, I am with you always, even to the end of the age" (Matthew 28:18–20). Jesus has been given all authority and He commissions you to go into your world and bring those whom you influence to the obedience of faith in Him.

For this task, the Lord has not left you comfortless. Nor has He left you powerless. He has given His Holy Spirit to equip you for the task. "But you shall receive power when the Holy Spirit has come upon you; and you shall be witnesses to Me in Jerusalem, and in all Judea and Samaria, and to the end of the earth" (Acts 1:8).

Of course, the devil will see to it that you are tempted to sin and tempted to be diverted from your walk with the Lord. However, you have the promise, "No temptation has overtaken you except such as is common to man; but God is faithful, who will not allow you to be tempted beyond what you are able, but with the temptation will also make the way of escape, that you may be able to bear it" (1 Corinthians 10:13).

Jesus himself has given you as His follower power over all of the power of the devil. "Behold, I give you the authority to trample on serpents and scorpions, and over all the power of the enemy, and nothing shall by any means hurt you. Nevertheless do not rejoice in this, that the spirits are subject to you, but rather rejoice because your names are written in heaven" (Luke 10:19–20). You are to recognize the fact that Satan is subject to you but you are to rejoice in the fact that salvation is yours through Christ.

Now you have taken ten preliminary yet major steps in your walk with the Lord Jesus. Where do you go from here? Just keep walking with Him, wherever and however He leads. The best counsel I could leave you is this: "But grow in the grace and knowledge of our Lord and Savior Jesus Christ. To Him be the glory both now and forever. Amen" (2 Peter 3:18).

TAKE A STEP OF ACTION!

❐ I am believing God's promises and I will continue to walk with Him wherever He leads me.

❐ Remember: "For we walk by faith, not by sight" (2 Corinthians 5:7).

STUDY GUIDE

Your Most Important Step

1. What is the most important step you can take in life? (p. 7)

2. According to John 3:16, what is the result of putting your faith in Jesus Christ? (p. 8)

3. According to Isaiah 59:2, what separates us from God? (p. 8)

4. Is eternal life a reward for our accomplishments or a gift from God? (p. 9)

5. What does it mean to commit yourself to Christ? (p. 9–10)

6. Have you personally turned from your sins and committed your life to Jesus Christ as your Savior and Lord?

Step One: Publicly Confess Your Faith in Christ

1. Salvation includes being saved from the _____ of our sins. What does Jesus say about the condition of the person who does not believe in Him? (p. 14)

2. What does it mean to be redeemed? What was the price of our redemption? (p. 15)

3. What is the ultimate assurance of salvation? (p. 16)

4. What does it mean to be saved by the grace of God? (p. 17)

5. What are the steps given to assurance of salvation? (p. 18–20)

6. Give three reasons why a public confession of Christ is important. (p. 23–24)

7. Have you publicly stated that you are trusting Jesus Christ as your Savior and following Him as your Lord?

Step Two: Follow Christ in Water Baptism

1. Why is water baptism called an "ordinance" of the church? (p. 26)

2. List three ways that baptism is a statement of your faith in Christ. (p. 28)

3. What are the three witnesses to our salvation spoken of in 1 John 5:8? Applying this verse, what does the author say bears witness to the world that we belong to Christ? (p. 28)

4. Have you been baptized in water as a testimony to the world of your union with Christ?

Step Three: Allow the Holy Spirit to Fill and Control You

1. What is the central work of the Holy Spirit? (p. 31)

2. What title does Jesus give to the Holy Spirit in John 16:13? (p. 32)

3. List the different fruits of the Spirit mentioned in Galatians 5:22–23. (p. 32)

4. According to Jesus in Acts 1:8, what would happen when the Holy Spirit came? (p. 33)

5. What three steps of preparation to being filled with the Holy Spirit does the author suggest? (p. 34–35)

6. Have you allowed the Holy Spirit to fill and control you?

Step Four: Turn from Every Known Sin

1. What separates us from fellowship with God? (p. 37)

2. How can we lead holy lives? (p. 38–39)

3. According to Hebrews 12, what is a sure evidence that God is dealing with us as His children? (p. 40)

4. What is "spiritual breathing"? (p. 41)

5. What formula for victory over temptation does Paul describe in Romans 6? (p. 41–42)

6. Have you asked the Holy Spirit to spotlight any and all sin in your life? Have you turned from all known sin and, by faith, received God's cleansing and forgiveness?

Step Five: Unite with a Strong Local Church

1. According to Acts 20:28, with what did God purchase the Church? (p. 43–44)

2. What illustration does Paul use in Ephesians 5 to describe the relationship between Christ and the Church? (p. 44–45)

3. What is the purpose of committed fellowship in a local church? (p. 46)

4. What characteristics does the author say you should look for in a God-honoring church? (p. 48)

5. Have you united with a Christ-exalting church and are you regularly fellowshiping there with your brothers and sisters in Christ?

Step Six: Lay the Proper Foundations

1. Who is the great foundation or "cornerstone" of the Christian's life? (p. 52)

2. List the six foundational principles found in Hebrews 6:1–2. (p. 52)

3. Is repentance merely an initial experience or a lifestyle? (p. 53)

4. When we think of repentance, most people think of repentance from sin. Is there anything else from which we should repent? (p. 53)

5. "God responds to _____" (p. 54). Do you agree with this statement?

6. What three baptisms are listed on page 54?

7. What is the difference in coming judgment for those who have placed their faith in Christ and those who have not placed their faith in Him? (p. 56–57)

8. Have you laid the proper foundation on which to build your life in Christ?

Step Seven: Let the Bible Speak to You

1. In the original language, 2 Timothy 3:16 says that "all scripture is God-breathed." (p. 60) What does that mean to you?

2. What is the importance of the Old Testament for us today? (p. 61).

3. In Joshua 1:8, what promise does the Bible give for those who meditate on it and obey its truths? (p. 62)

4. On pages 62–63, several suggestions are given to help you begin an effective program of Bible study. What are some of those suggestions?

5. Have you established a daily time to allow the Lord to speak to you through His Word?

Step Eight: Talk to God in Prayer

1. Why can we approach God with boldness? (p. 65–66)

2. List at least two reasons why we should pray. (p. 66–67)

3. What are seven attitudes that should be reflected in our praying? (p. 67–68)

4. What model did Jesus give His disciples for effective praying? (p. 68–69)

5. Prayer is often a literal though unseen war. According to Ephesians 6, how should we prepare for spiritual warfare? (p. 69)

6. Are you developing an intimate relationship with God through prayer?

Step Nine: Reach Others for Jesus

1. According to the author, what is the highest privilege in life? (p. 73)

2. According to the author, witnessing for Jesus Christ is not only our privilege but our _____. (p. 73)

3. In 2 Corinthians 5:20, what title are Christians given? (p. 74)

4. List four qualifications for being an effective witness for Christ. (p. 74–76)

5. What are some ways to break the "silence barrier"? (p. 76–77)

6. How can you be involved in God's global plan? (p. 77–78)

7. Are you consistently sharing your faith in Jesus Christ with others?

Step Ten: Trust God's Promises

1. Jesus has promised never to leave us. This is the promise of His _____ (p. 82). Because He is always with us, all of life has a _____ running through it. (p. 82)

2. According to Romans 8:29, what is God's ultimate purpose for your life? (p. 83) What promise from the Bible assures you that God will accomplish His purpose in you? (p. 83)

3. One of the titles given to God is "The-Lord-Will-Provide" (Genesis 22:14). His greatest provision was the offering of

His Son, Jesus Christ, as the sacrifice for our sins. List some other ways in which the Lord provides for us. (p. 83–84)

4. Who has been given to us so we may have power to live lives that are pleasing to God? (p. 84)

5. Are you believing God's promises? Will you continue to walk with Him wherever He leads you?

INDEX OF SCRIPTURE REFERENCES

DAVID SHIBLEY

David Shibley is president and founder of Global Advance, a missions ministry equipping and resourcing national church leaders to reach their own people and surrounding peoples with the gospel. With over a quarter century of fruitful ministry in over 30 nations, he also travels extensively throughout the United States speaking in behalf of world evangelism.

In addition to his ministry with Global Advance, Mr. Shibley serves on eight missions boards and is a member of the far-reaching U.S. Lausanne Committee on World Evangelization. He is the author of eight books and numerous articles.

A graduate of John Brown University in Arkansas, and Southwestern Baptist Theological Seminary, he holds an honorary doctorate from ORU. He and his wife, Naomi, have two sons.

For more information contact:

Global Advance

P.O. Box 742077

Dallas, TX 75374-2077

Also by David Shibley

HEAVEN'S HEROES

REAL LIFE STORIES FROM
HISTORY'S GREATEST MISSIONARIES

"God had an only Son and He was a missionary. . . ." With these words, David Livingstone confirmed that he, too, would spend his life telling people in far-off lands about the love of God.

David Livingstone is one of 22 men and women whose exciting adventures will be enjoyed by the whole family in this inspiring book. As you read each of these wonderful stories, aloud during family times or on your own, you will see how you can also reach out to your world through deeds and prayer to tell others the good news about Jesus and His love.

Paperback • 144 pages • $7.99
ISBN-13: 978-0-89221-255-2
ISBN-10: 0-89221-255-1

Available at Christian bookstores nationwide

Dr. Herbert V. Guenther is Head of the Department of Far Eastern Studies at the University of Saskatchewan. Through his numerous translations and articles he has made major contributions to the understanding and accessibility of Tibetan Buddhism in the West. His books include *The Jewel Ornament of Liberation*, *The Life and Teachings of Naropa*, *Treasures on the Tibetan Middle Way*, *Buddhist Philosophy in Theory and Practice*, and *Tantric View of Life*.

Rev. Leslie S. Kawamura is a Buddhist priest of the Pure Land School. He received a Master's degree from Kyoto University and is a teaching fellow at the University of Saskatchewan. He has also translated *Golden Zephyr*.